BALANCE YOUR AGNI

NOW AGE
ESSENTIALS

BALANCE

ESSENTIAL

YOUR

AYURVEDA

AGNI

CLAIRE PAPHITIS

POP PRESS

Published in 2020 by Pop Press an imprint of Ebury Publishing,

20 Vauxhall Bridge Road,
London SW1V 2SA

Pop Press is part of the Penguin Random House group of companies
whose addresses can be found at global.penguinrandomhouse.com

First published by Pop Press in 2020

www.penguin.co.uk

Design by Imagist

A CIP catalogue record for this book is available from the British Library

ISBN 9781529107296

The information in this book has been compiled by way of general
guidance in relation to the specific subjects addressed, but is not a
substitute and not to be relied on for medical, healthcare, pharmaceutical
or other professional advice on specific circumstances and in specific
locations. Please consult your GP before changing, stopping or starting
any medical treatment or changing your diet. So far as the author is aware
the information given is correct and up to date as at May 2020. Practice,
laws and regulations all change, and the reader should obtain up-to-date
professional advice on any such issues. The author and publishers
disclaim, as far as the law allows, any liability arising directly or indirectly
from the use, or misuse, of the information contained in this book.

Typeset in 9/12 pt Neuzeit Office Pro
by Integra Software Services Pvt. Ltd, Pondicherry

Printed and bound in Great Britain by Clays Ltd, Elcograf S.p.A.

MIX
Paper from
responsible sources
FSC® C018179

Contents

FOR MY MOTHER – WITH MY
DEEPEST GRATITUDE.

Introducing the Power of Ayurveda

Ayurveda has become something of a buzzword in recent times, finding its way into food writing, beauty, lifestyle, wellness retreats and all manner of health and well-being outlets, enabling people to harness its powerful benefits in a multitude of ways. Ayurveda takes a 360-degree holistic approach to our physical and mental health through digestion, nutrition, lifestyle, nature and universal energy. Although it finds itself in a very busy market of well-being practices, it stands out because it is the most beautiful and complete understanding of the laws of nature and the Universe. It is a discipline with ancient roots that teaches us how to achieve that very modern goal: mind–body balance.

The Power of Ayurveda

Ayurveda is the sister science of yoga and it is traditional
in India to study Ayurveda first – because it is believed
that only when our body is ready and in balance can we
take up the spiritual practice of yoga. In the twenty-first
century our lives are incredibly busy and overstimulated,
yet despite advances in modern medicine we still get sick.
We might 'have it all' as far as consumables go, but our
souls are searching for something else and our mental
health is suffering. In a culture of quick fixes and
immediate satisfaction, Ayurveda is reassuringly enduring,
based on more than 5,000 years of tried-and-tested
knowledge. It is a wisdom based on creating balance and
it offers a slow and gentle method of creating equilibrium,
based on a little self-discipline and delayed gratification.
No bad thing to counter the fast-paced urgency of
modern life.

How Ayurveda Can Help You

In this book, I hope to guide you gently through an introduction to authentic Ayurveda, showing you how to implement key principles in your everyday life. As a qualified practitioner, I see patients from all walks of life who are suffering with many different disorders, ranging from skin conditions through to hormonal and fertility disorders. But you can also use the power of Ayurveda to help yourself find a balanced way of eating, boost your mood, improve your sleep and concentration, increase your capacity for compassion and forgiveness and find peace and calm within. The beauty of this ancient Indian medicinal practice is that it addresses the root causes of a disorder and works by removing these causative factors rather than by simply masking the symptoms with medication. Although every individual and the cause of their illness will be unique, my approach to treating all these patients is the same: balance your Agni (digestive fire) and calm the dosha(s).

I will explain the key principles of exactly what this means and showcase the everyday power of Ayurveda through its potential to not only change the way you eat for the better but how, by following a few simple practices, it can bring about real and lasting transformations to your overall well-being.

You will learn ways to recognise how well your Agni (digestive fire) is working, why it is so important to your health and how to ensure it stays balanced. I will help you to uncover a novel approach to understanding the 'characteristics' of the doshas so you can more easily recognise imbalances in your own body and discover what you need to do to bring yourself back into perfect balance. You will learn simple daily practices that are easy to implement and will bring a boost to your emotional and mental health, improve your energy levels, soothe skin conditions, balance hormones, help you maintain a good metabolism and reduce stress and anxiety.

I hope this book will ignite in you a lifelong interest in Ayurveda and that after reading it, you will feel empowered to incorporate these simple practices into your day-to-day life. Ayurveda has blessed me with a health and contentment that I never thought I would find and I hope very much it will bring the same to you.

IMPORTANT NOTE: Please consult your doctor or a qualified practitioner before changing your diet or introducing new substances to your daily routine, particularly if you are on any medication or have any existing health conditions.

What is Ayurveda?

The word 'Ayurveda' comes from two Sanskrit words: *Ayur*, meaning 'life', and *Veda*, meaning 'knowledge/science of'. So to study Ayurveda is to be a lifelong student of the 'Knowledge of Life'. Ayurveda has its roots in ancient India and encompasses both philosophy and science. In fact, it is the world's oldest medical healing system, reaching back as far back as 10,000 years, and has eight different branches of medicine: general medicine, surgery, paediatrics, geriatrics, obstetrics, gynaecology, ophthalmology and medicine of the ears, nose and throat.

Where It All Began

Thousands of years ago, the daily meditation practice of the Rishis or sages of India enabled them to receive the knowledge and wisdom of the Universe. Through their meditations, they perceived the relationship between human beings and the Universe, and how this cosmic energy is present in all living things. Their understanding evolved over thousands of years and was traditionally transmitted orally from teacher to student, until around 5,000 years ago, when the earliest texts were put into writing. Sanskrit has a melodious oral tradition, often poetic, so the texts are written in Sanskrit verses or *slokas* and have been passed down, unchanged, through countless generations.

In Ayurvedic philosophy, human beings are viewed as a microcosm of the Universe because we are made up of and interact with the five basic principles of all creation: the elements of Ether (or space), Air, Water, Fire and Earth. The Rishis understood that all things were created from these five elements. It is said that from a state of un-manifested consciousness came the micro vibrations of the soundless 'aum' or 'Om' – a word or sound that you may be familiar with from yoga or meditation practice. The vibrations from this enduring sound began in the Ether, or empty space, and from here subtle movements created vibrations within the Ether – which became Air. This movement began to create friction and heat – an energy which formed an intense light that would become Fire. Through the heat of this Fire, unseen elements dissolved and liquefied into Water. As the Water cooled and became solid, Earth was created.

As you will discover during the course of this book, these five elements of Ether, Air, Water, Fire and Earth govern all our physical and mental processes. If you are wondering how Air or Fire or Ether are present in your own body, allow me to elaborate a little further.

The Ether element represents space. There are many ways this manifests within our bodies - in the mouth and nasal cavities, for example, or within the gastrointestinal (GI) tract or the space in our blood vessels.

The Air element is visible as movement in the spaces - pulsations of the heart, for example, or the expansion and contraction of our lungs, and movements of the intestines and muscles. Any movement in the body is governed by the Air element.

The Fire element is responsible for digestion, sight and intelligence. Our metabolism and digestive enzymes are all governed by the element of Fire. It is the heat that powers our bodies.

The Water element is perhaps the simplest of the bodily elements to understand. We know our bodies are about 60 per cent water and it can be found in the digestive juices, our saliva and any mucous membranes.

The Earth element is the fifth and final element in Ayurveda - representing the solid structure of our bones, nails and cartilage.

The five elements provide an individual blueprint for health and longevity, but only if we can understand and interpret how they each interact within our bodies and the environment around us. Having this awareness and intuition will become important as you begin (or continue) your journey into adopting Ayurveda into your daily life. And remember, because we are this microcosm of the Universe, there is a constant interaction between our internal and external environments, and often they are doing battle with one another. External factors such as the weather, the seasons, work stress or issues with family and friends will all create disturbances that affect how the five elements within our bodies interact, but we can learn to recognise the signs and how to create balance.

'Like increases like'

We might not be as in touch with nature and our inner wisdom as our ancestors were thousands of years ago, but it's still there in all of us and we all do things that benefit our bodies intuitively without even realising it.

Here's an example of how we apply the Ayurvedic principle of 'like increases like' every day without even thinking. Imagine it's the middle of autumn and outside the conditions are cold and windy and the ground is hard and dry. What do you do? Head out in a T-shirt and sandals with an ice-cold drink and a salad? No. That's because we intuitively know that doing so would increase the Air element in our bodies and make us feel colder and drier. We know instinctively that like increases like, so we reach for hot drinks, hot soups, our cosiest jumpers, warm baths and soothing oils to counteract the effects of the dry, cold, windy season.

In this way, we turn to food, drink and activities that have opposite qualities to create balance – and by doing so, we are already practising Ayurveda. We have intuitively understood this basic principle of creating balance through altering diet and lifestyle habits in accordance with our external environment. As you begin your own journey into understanding Ayurveda, keep in mind the principle of 'like increases like' and ensure that you look for the opposite qualities of whatever is disrupting your equilibrium in order to maintain balance.

I will explore this principle in more detail later in the book, particularly in reference to how we can take better care of ourselves at different times of the year, but first I would like to introduce you to some of the key concepts in Ayurveda: Agni, Ojas and the three doshas – Vata, Pitta and Kapha.

Agni: Your Fire Power

Agni is a Sanskrit word that literally translates as 'fire'. When we refer to Agni in Ayurveda we are talking about our digestive fire – quite literally the power or strength of your digestion. According to Ayurveda, Agni is the life force of intelligence within each cell, tissue and system within the body. Solar energy is the source of any sort of conversion in any living thing and Agni represents this solar energy, or 'fire power' if you like, in human beings.

The Ayurvedic concept of Agni as a foundation for good health is now being supported by modern medicine, as scientists have discovered the importance of gut health and the link between our gut and not just our physical well-being but our mental health. It might be a concept that is more than 5,000 years old, but when our modern and busy lives start to overwhelm us, when we get sick or just feel a bit below par, we can look to Ayurveda for the answers – it teaches us in a most beautiful and thorough way exactly why our digestive health is so important and what we can do to look after it.

In Ayurveda what we call Agni encompasses many of the modern buzzwords that now surround gut health, such as 'digestive enzymes', 'probiotics', 'digestive flora', 'the microbiome' and so on. There is a very famous saying in Ayurveda which comes from one of the ancient Sanskrit texts; it is *Roga Sarvapi Mandagnaue* and it means 'every disorder is the result of an impaired Agni'.

Yes. You read that correctly. *Every disorder.*

So this important verse is telling us that an impaired digestive fire will create imbalance and disease; in fact, it means that all disease originates from a poor digestive fire. This concept and the importance of caring for your Agni is the one thing I would encourage you to take away from this book above anything else.

I will explain in more detail and as simply as possible exactly what the Agni does and why it is so important for our overall health. I hope that by understanding the concept more fully, you will feel empowered to take charge of balancing your own Agni and improving your health and immunity.

The Functions of Agni

Here are just a few of the bodily functions Agni is responsible for:

· transforming our food into nutrition and waste;
· digesting, absorbing and assimilating nutrients;
· maintaining our metabolism;
· the clarity of our complexions;
· regulating our body temperature;
· giving us the power of thought and mental clarity;
· the production of Ojas (don't worry – I will explain this term on pages 38–9).

We will all experience an imbalanced Agni at various points in our lives, but the key is to recognise this and make changes so that it doesn't stay imbalanced for too long.

The health of your Agni can be categorised into four different states:

Too High - Tikshana Agni

Too Low - Manda Agni

Impaired - Vishama Agni

Balanced - Sama Agni (the Holy Grail!)

If it is balanced ('Sama Agni'), the food, drink and even emotions we feed into our bodies can be processed correctly; nutrients are absorbed into the tissues and waste is sent out of the body. If it is not functioning as it should, we will start to experience unwanted symptoms.

The state of our Agni is inevitably affected when its functions are disrupted by a poor diet, poor lifestyle choices, emotional disturbances, food poisoning or even the seasonal changes and outside weather conditions. By learning to recognise these imbalances and how best to address them, we can rebalance our Agni relatively quickly. However, if we continue to ignore the warning signs, the Agni will continue to be impaired and it will take longer and more effort to repair.

Recognising Imbalance

Some typical indications that Agni is disturbed and needs attention include:

- low energy, weakness, or fatigue;
- lack of appetite;
- over-active appetite;
- indigestion, gas, bloating, excessive wind, sluggish digestion;
- acid reflux, heartburn, gurgling sounds in stomach;
- constipation or very loose stools;
- a sense of heaviness after eating;
- brain fog, headaches;
- frequently congested sinuses/chest;
- white coating on tongue;
- emotional disturbances, particularly fear, anxiety, anger or depression.

You could have one or many tell-tale symptoms from the above list. These symptoms may only occur every so often or you may have experienced them for a long time. Either way, they signal an issue with your Agni and lead to the accumulation of toxins and the disruption of the three bodily doshas – Vata, Pitta and Kapha (see page 46) – as well as creating blockages in the channels of the body (known as the Srotas) and the stagnation of emotions. Essentially, it could mean the disruption of your entire system!

The Thirteen Agni

There are thirteen main Agnis in the body, each with specific functions. However, they fall into three groups:

Jathara Agni assists in 'cooking' the food to break it down and separate out that which can be used as nourishment and nutrition, and that which needs to be eliminated.

Bhuta Agni receive the already broken-down food from the Jathara Agni and process it further into five sub-groups to nourish the five elements of the body: Ether, Air, Water, Fire and Earth. When we say we need to 'cleanse our livers' what our body is probably telling us is to balance our Bhuta Agni!

Dhatu Agni reside in the seven tissues or 'dhatu'. These Agnis receive the broken-down food and pass it down through the seven tissue levels. This process (from the time we eat the food to the time the last part of the nourishment reaches the seventh tissue level) takes thirty-five days! This is why it can sometimes take a little time before you start to see real changes to your well-being. Be patient – it will be worth it.

How Imbalanced Agni leads to Disease

Once nutrition has been extracted and sent to the seven tissues, what is left is waste product or toxins. In Ayurveda we call this 'Ama'.

Our bodies are very clever and sophisticated machines that have all the necessary functions we require to keep us healthy. If we eat a bad piece of chicken, for example, our body knows within hours that this is toxic to our system and it expels it in ways that I am sure we have all experienced. In a similar way, when the digestive fire is working well, it recognises and processes Ama by sending it to the normal channels of elimination. There is no need for extreme 'cleanses' – just look after the digestive fire and your body will take care of eliminating what shouldn't be there!

Unfortunately, when the digestive fire is imbalanced, the Ama will remain in the body and begin to circulate in the tissues, eventually manifesting as disease. We can sometimes physically see this Ama manifest in the first tissue level as eczema symptoms or acne, for example. Alternatively, if it has gone deeper into the tissues, you may suffer from arthritis and joint pain, a sign Ama has reached the Asthi dhatu or bone level. Perhaps you have irregular or painful periods or symptoms of endometriosis – in this case, the Ama is causing blockages.

Good nutrition, a healthy Agni and the management of Ama will give balance to the body and mind and help protect you from disease.

Caring for Your Agni

There are so many benefits to having a balanced Agni: you will find you sleep better, your mind is clearer, you will feel energised by a good metabolism and maintain a steady weight through eating warm, nutritious food that you can digest well. When Agni is balanced your immunity will be strong, you will have pleasant thoughts and feel calm and positive in yourself.

I would like you to practise a little visualisation with me to help you understand the Agni in your stomach. I often have a candle burning during consultations and I ask patients to imagine that the flame represents the Agni in their stomach. When hunger comes, the flame ignites. Just like a real fire, for the Agni this represents a call for more fuel, i.e. food!

By listening to this call and eating a cooked, warm and easily digestible meal, the flame can burn steadily without producing too much smoke or ash (think of the smoke and ash as being the Ama or toxins). When we hear the call for fuel but consume cold or raw foods and salads, it is like throwing iced water onto the little fire; it simply cannot function properly. The food goes 'uncooked' by the fire and becomes more like sludge (Ama again!).

Another common pitfall (and one that I have certainly unwittingly fallen victim to in the past) is to have a glass of water or a cup of coffee instead of food, or simply to ignore the hunger entirely and so starve the fire of any fuel at all. This is just as damaging for the Agni as eating the wrong kind of foods. If you picture again the little flame and what happens when we pour water on it or stop adding any wood or fuel, the fire simply goes out. If the Agni is weakened by these sorts of practices, it cannot perform its job correctly when we do finally stop and eat something.

While many of us may be able to ignore hunger or satisfy it with a glass of water or a cup of tea, some of us will be very familiar with the term 'hangry'. This is when hunger comes and must be satisfied immediately – or else we cannot be responsible for our actions! This is another sign of the Agni not functioning correctly. It is healthy and normal to experience a moderate amount of hunger at appropriate times of the day (with, let's say, a break of four to six hours between meals), but when we experience this intense hunger and need for immediate food, it is a sign of the Agni burning too brightly ('tikshana Agni'). The digestive fire has become out of control and we need to take steps to calm it down by making adjustments to our diet – usually by reducing our intake of heating foods such as tomatoes, chilli, pickles, vinegars, cheese, red meat and red wine.

'If the Agni is balanced, one can digest rocks' – so goes the Ayurvedic saying. Just as it can burn too brightly, the Agni can also be sluggish and slow ('manda Agni'). While the rise in food intolerances can be partly explained by the way our food is stored and produced these days, we cannot ignore the role a poorly functioning Agni has to play. A balanced digestive fire will allow you the freedom to enjoy a wide variety of food groups, but if it is weak you can suffer from bloating, wind, digestive discomfort or allergic reactions.

Understanding Your Digestion – how healthy is Your Agni?

So what are the signs of a healthy and balanced Agni? There are a number of signals that we can tune in to, which can help us recognise when our Agni is working optimally and when perhaps it needs some closer attention.

Digestion will always be a key indicator. Do you have to avoid certain foods because they make you bloated or feel uncomfortable or lethargic after eating? Do you suffer with irregular bowel movements?

Wind, belching, indigestion, a gurgling stomach, heartburn and acid reflux are all signs to watch out for. If they start becoming a frequent issue, it is time to take action and examine what and how you are eating, and asses the state of your Agni.

One of the easiest things to spot is whether you have an appetite at all. A complete lack of appetite suggests Agni is very low, whereas a normal appetite occurs at decent intervals during the day – something like two or three times per day – and creates a pleasant anticipation for food rather than 'hanger' and an out-of-control Agni.

Depending on your dosha, you may not always feel the need to eat something in the morning. If you are a Vata type, you may not want to eat at all, but it might be wise to have a little something to ground you. If you are Kapha, you should opt for something light. If you are Pitta, you will need a meal to sustain you through the morning. Make a mental note of your hunger over a period of five to seven days. Is it more pronounced at certain times of the day? Does it behave differently when you are at work versus home or when you are under stress?

A good appreciation of all six tastes is also important (see pages 71–3). Often we have a tendency to rely excessively on sweet, sour and salty tastes and shy away from foods with more pungent, astringent or bitter tastes. A healthy craving is one that goes away when you consume that taste. If the craving does not subside or continues for more than a day or two, it is a sure sign at least one of the doshas is imbalanced. Check in with your cravings and refer to pages 71–3 for more information on the six tastes and how they relate to imbalances and the doshas.

My Top Five Tips to Balance Your Agni

Remember to think of your Agni as an energetic force, a 'fire' that doesn't burn excessively brightly, nor smoulder and smoke – or worse, go out entirely! The quality of Agni varies depending upon your dosha and other factors such as the quality and type of foods you are eating. Following these simple guidelines will help to ensure you look after your Agni:

- Avoid raw, cold foods.
- Treat your Agni to warm, cooked and nourishing foods. Vegetables should always be cooked – whether that be sautéed, steamed, roasted or put into a stir-fry. Consuming cooked foods aids the further 'cooking' process that the Agni has to perform.
- If you feel true hunger, this is your Agni waking up. Eat something! Don't substitute food with a glass of water or a cup of coffee. The liquid will only dampen the Agni back down, meaning it has to work harder when you do eventually eat.
- Avoid drinking very cold water or putting ice in your drinks. This will only help to extinguish the Agni. Try water at room temperature or warm.
- Use herbs and spices in your cooking to increase Agni before and during meals.

Home Remedies to Balance Your Agni and Improve Your Digestive Fire

In Ayurvedic cooking, it is believed that using spices will support a long life by aiding digestion and ensuring that more energy and fewer toxins are taken into the body. This doesn't mean chilli spice; instead, think of spices and herbs such as cumin, coriander, black pepper, long pepper, liquorice, fennel, fenugreek, nutmeg, cinnamon, cardamom, cloves, parsley and basil.

Cooking with spices will help increase the secretion of saliva and stimulate the digestive enzymes in the stomach and intestines (i.e. fire up your Agni!). Using these spices will also help to prevent gas. Hing (also known as asafoetida) is particularly good for this and you only need a pinch. Fennel is another herb commonly consumed after meals to prevent gas, discomfort and fatigue.

It is important to remember that undigested food is broken down by fermentation rather than digestion, and fermentation is what produces gas and toxins. The intestines then absorb these gases.

CUMIN, CORIANDER AND FENNEL CHOORNA (FOR CALMING TIKSHANA AGNI)

Tikshana Agni can mean the digestive fire has become excessive and you may experience heartburn, acid reflux and other burning sensations. Or it may be that you have a tendency to 'stress eat' or feel you are constantly getting hungry. If this sounds like you, try this simple home remedy after meals for a week or two until your symptoms subside.

100g/2oz cumin seeds
100g/2oz coriander seeds
100g/2oz fennel seeds
50g/2oz fenugreek seeds

1. Lightly toast each batch of seeds in a dry frying pan for 30–60 seconds until fragrant. Toast each type separately as they will not all take the same amount of time to cook.
2. Grind to a fine powder in a coffee grinder. Sieve and grind again.
3. Mix well and store in an airtight container.

Dosage: Adults can take 1 tsp of the mixture in 50–100ml/2–3½fl oz hot water after meals.

CUMIN AND HONEY (FOR BALANCING ALL TYPES OF AGNI)

This recipe is extremely effective for balancing any type of Agni, whether you are Vata, Pitta or Kapha. It is always my 'go to' when I am feeling a bit below par. It is gentle enough to take daily but also very effective at balancing Agni and dislodging toxins.

100g/2oz cumin seeds
raw, organic honey

1. Toast the seeds lightly in a dry frying pan.
2. Grind the seeds to a fine powder in a coffee grinder
3. Store in an airtight container.

Dosage: Adults can take 1 tsp of the powder with ½ tsp of honey before meals. Children aged five and above can be given ¼ tsp of cumin powder and ½–1 tsp honey after their meal. Agave syrup can be used for those who can't tolerate honey.

GINGER, LIME AND SALT (FOR PERKING UP MANDA AGNI)

For when digestion is feeling slow and a bit sluggish, this recipe will give your Agni a kick up the proverbial!

Take a small slice of fresh root ginger and squeeze over a few drops of lime juice and a pinch of salt. Chew this slowly before meals. It will help to fire up the Agni, ready to digest food more efficiently.

Ojas: Taking Care of You

Ojas are responsible for our strength, vitality and immunity – they protect us from disease. Immunity and Ojas can be broadly thought of as the same thing. Immunity is the reason 100 people can be infected with the same disease and some are able to fight it off while others are not. Ojas are seated in the heart – they are the reason a mother may be able to care for her sick children without getting sick herself.

On a psychological level, Ojas are the highest form of compassion and love. A person with strong Ojas will exude a sense of calm. They will glow with a health and vitality that comes not only from the physical health of their body but from a spiritual energy of the mind and higher consciousness.

To increase your Ojas, you need to able to remove the ego and move past unconscious attitudes to life and to others. We talk now about staying 'woke'. This is a move in the right direction, but saying it or thinking it is not enough: it needs to come from the heart. Acts of unselfish kindness and love are how we can build and strengthen Ojas in our bodies, and by doing so we will strengthen our natural immunity.

Food is also key. After the seven dhatus or tissues have been nourished, the very last part of this 35-day process is for 'eight drops of Ojas' to be produced. We have already looked at how our Agni needs to be working healthily and how we need to eat in order for the process to be completed adequately so that all seven tissues receive what they need to function correctly, but there is an eighth part of the process! This is the creation of Ojas.

Think of it this way: you can buy a ready-made sandwich from a supermarket and eat it on the run or you can prepare a sandwich at home, take it to work with you and sit down and eat it calmly in the park on your lunchbreak. The ingredients are the same: bread, filling, butter – but the energy of the sandwich that was created at home with love and which is consumed slowly and mindfully is the one that will have the best chance of turning into Ojas in the body.

Build Your Ojas and Share Compassion and Love

Our lives are busy. There are so many demands on our time coming from all areas, which mean that we often put food and eating right at the bottom of our list of priorities. Yet in virtually any gathering or celebration, what is nearly always at the centre? Food! When we go on a romantic date with a loved one, throw a birthday party, a wedding, whatever the occasion – food takes centre stage.

We have known for centuries that good food is more than just fuel; it is love. If we want to enjoy good health, physical energy and mental well-being in order to prosper and flourish, we have to make the time to eat correctly. Next time you are feeling anxious or jittery about work or irritated with your partner, next time something has upset you or when you just need some 'me' time, take a deep breath, go into the kitchen and make a simple meal. It doesn't have to be complicated and it doesn't matter if you think you can cook or not. Roast a chicken, prepare some vegetables or make a soup, stir together some simple lentils with spices and coconut milk. Take a few moments to admire the ingredients. Smell them, taste them. Let your mind and emotions be calm and still as you put your energy into making a meal that will nourish you and your loved ones. Turn the focus away from yourself and pour love into preparing that meal. Then invite your friends or family to join you. Turn off your phones and the television and sit down and eat together. The Ojas will flow. Forget anything else you may have read. This is Ayurveda.

PRANA AND GUNAS: OUR LIFE FORCE

There are a further three subtle energies or 'gunas' that are responsible for influencing the qualities of the mind. These are sattva, rajas and tamas. The three gunas are the energetic states that Prana (our life force) exists in. They also rely on a balanced Agni, good nutrition and Ojas. The three gunas are:

Sattva – compassion, calmness, creativity, love. The essence of pure light and spiritual purpose.

Rajas – movement, power, prestige, anger, ambition, desire.

Tamas – depression, sluggishness, darkness, laziness.

Just as we can have a dominance of one of the doshas in our bodies (see the chapter 'The Doshas and You'), so too can we have a lack or excess of the three gunas. The good news is that it's possible to consciously change the levels within our bodies and minds through good nutrition, strengthening our Ojas and changing the influence that external objects, people and thoughts have on us.

We will see and experience the world according to which of the gunas is most dominant at any particular time. If Sattva is more predominant, a person will view the world around them as a positive and joyful place to be. If there is more Tamas, the person will perceive the world as a negative, depressing and broken place. Tamas types tend to also be highly egotistical.

By increasing Sattva, we can reduce the levels of Rajas and Tamas. This takes conscious effort but it can be done in a similar way to how we build our Ojas: through love and compassion and acting unselfishly, by eating fresh, home-cooked foods and surrounding ourselves with people and experiences that bring positive energy to our lives.

Draw a line down the centre of a piece of paper. On the left-hand side, make a list of people and activities that bring joy and pleasure to your heart. On the other side, list people, activities or situations that feel negative or destructive to you. Focus on letting go of and avoiding the things listed on the right side and increasing your exposure to the things listed on the left. This can be done!

Avoid heavy and processed foods and excessive amounts of alcohol, as these create more Tamas energy. Reducing Tamas is probably easier to do than reducing Rajas. I think many of us live somewhere in the realm of Rajas energy: we have ambition and desire, we look for external validation from others, and so on. And that's ok, because to be truly Sattvic means to be enlightened – and this is only for the very few. We can all nonetheless make a conscious effort to increase our own Sattvic qualities, knowing that increasing our own will then have a knock-on effect on the lives and well-being of others. I like to think of that old saying 'when you smile, the world smiles with you'. When you smile at a stranger or have a kind word to say to someone, not only do you increase your own levels of Sattva, but you will be increasing theirs too, and perhaps they will pass that on to someone else they meet that day and so the good energy spreads. It can really be as simple as that.

The Doshas
and You

The three doshas are called Vata, Pitta and Kapha and they are made up of the five elements that are found in all living things: Ether, Air, Fire, Water and Earth, i.e. the building blocks of all life. Each dosha is a combination of two of these elements as follows:

Vata = Ether + Air

Pitta = Fire + Water

Kapha = Water + Earth

We have already looked at how these five elements can be understood as physical elements in the body (see page 9); however, the doshas govern not only our physical make-up but the way we think and act. When I first began studying Ayurveda, my teacher gave an analogy about the three doshas being sent to build a bridge. This analogy helped me to understand the characteristics of the three doshas and how they can either aggravate each other and cause chaos, or work together as a trilogy in perfect harmony and balance. I have expanded on it and hope it helps you get to know Vata, Pitta and Kapha a little better too.

Meet the Doshas

The three doshas, Vata, Pitta and Kapha, are put in charge of building a new bridge. Vata is first out the blocks. She has a burst of energy at the start of this project and is blessed with the creativity and imagination to build something truly beautiful. She flits through a notebook of a hundred different designs that she has started to sketch out – she stayed up till 2am drawing them, but, being Vata, none are completely finished. She starts building the bridge one way but then changes her mind. She leaves half-built bridges all over the city. Then she disappears for days to go on a yoga retreat and take up pottery classes. Creative and free-spirited, she can't be held down in one place with one task for very long.

Enter Pitta. Pitta's sharp mind quickly discerns what must be done and, in military fashion, she has soon drawn up a careful plan, set budgets and recruited a workforce ready to build the bridge. Everything is carefully controlled but Pitta's perfectionism soon means her stress levels are through the roof. Before long, she is feeling hot, bothered and ready to explode at any moment. Just then, Vata returns.

'Where have you been?' exclaims Pitta. 'You left me to do everything! You can't just disappear when you feel like it – there is work to be done and deadlines to keep!'

To which Vata replies, 'I had to go find myself and be free of all these deadlines. But what have you done with my beautiful designs? And why are you shouting at me? I was all relaxed from my yoga retreat and now I feel very unsettled and anxious!'

They continue winding each other up. Pitta prods and pushes. Vata becomes increasingly agitated, like a whirlwind spinning out of control. Vata is just about to turn and run away when Kapha saunters in, only three weeks late ...

'What's all this fuss?' says Kapha. 'We had better sit down and have some tea and cake. Everyone will feel better then. Come, have a little rest and we can think about making the bridge tomorrow. Or maybe the day after ... '

Vata and Pitta sit down. They have a cup of tea and some cake. Vata has calmed down now. Pitta's face is no longer red and angry. Kapha is wondering if there is time for a quick snooze ...

The next day, refreshed and rejuvenated by Kapha's calming presence, Vata draws up some new plans, Pitta puts them into action and Kapha keeps the whole work force happy with her delicious food and tea breaks.

Perhaps you recognise elements of yourself or your friends and family in these descriptions? Which bridge builder do you relate to the most?

Don't be put off by the descriptions – Pitta doesn't always mean fiery and angry, Kapha is not always sitting around eating cake and Vata isn't always flitting off somewhere when things get too much – but can you see how easy it is for the doshas to get out of balance? And, equally, how simple it can be to find balance again by bringing qualities that have the opposite effect: Kapha needs the energy of

Vata to stop her becoming too lazy. Pitta needs Kapha's calming nature to stop her getting too wound up. Vata and Kapha both need Pitta to bring a sense of order and get things done.

It is the same with our bodies. The delicate balance of the three doshas is in a constant state of flux and can be thrown off by the seasons, the weather, the time of day and by an excess of aggravating foods or activities. The aim in Ayurveda is to try to keep all three in balance. If you have a predominance of Vata, you want to maintain that energy and creativity without becoming flighty and anxious. A Pitta type values intelligence, drive, organisation and leadership, but needs to avoid emotions boiling over into anger, control and jealousy. If you are mostly Kapha, the challenge is making sure your soothing, calming nature doesn't allow you to slide into laziness and over-eating.

Finding Your Dosha

In Ayurveda, every individual has a unique constitution made up of a mixture of the three doshas, a bit like the notion of DNA – it's just a different way of looking at the building blocks. You may be 50 per cent Vata, 30 per cent Pitta and 20 per cent Kapha, for example.

The basic constitution ('prakruti') of each individual is determined at conception. At the time of fertilisation, the combinations of bodily Ether, Air, Fire, Water and Earth that manifest in the parents' bodies will go on to determine the constitution of their child.

There are seven main types of constitution (or mind-body type):

1. Vata: Vata dosha is very dominant, with smaller amounts of the other two doshas present.

2. Pitta: Pitta dosha is very dominant, with a small amount of the other two doshas present.

3. Kapha: Kapha dosha is very dominant with a small amount of the other two doshas present.

4. Vata-Pitta: Vata and Pitta are present in roughly equal amounts, for example, making up around 45 per cent each while the remaining 10 per cent is Kapha.

5. Pitta-Kapha: Pitta and Kapha are the dominant doshas, with a small amount of Vata.

6. Vata-Kapha: Vata and Kapha are dominant, with a small amount of Pitta.

7. Vata-Pitta-Kapha: meaning tri-doshic. Lucky you! Each dosha is present in equal proportions. Very few of us are fortunate enough to be made this way or to be able to sustain a perfect balance, but if this is your prakruti and you can keep it in balance, you will enjoy a long and healthy life!

What is My Dosha?

This is often one of the first questions a patient will ask me. Trying to figure it out on your own or through quizzes can be confusing, because we are often such a varied mix of all three – and there can be many external factors affecting the natural state of the doshas in your body at any one time.

In contrast to our prakruti, which represents our inborn constitution, 'vikruti' represents the current state of doshas, or, in other words, the deviation from our true prakruti. As one indulges in incorrect foods, is subject to environmental changes, poor lifestyle habits and so on, the doshas can either increase or decrease, causing fluctuations in our bodies which impact on our physical and mental health.

The complexity of figuring out your dosha is often what causes people to give up on Ayurveda at the first hurdle. But I want to reassure you that although the dosha is a key principle of Ayurveda and one that it is helpful to understand, you don't need to place too much importance on it at the start of your journey. After all, you wouldn't go to see your GP at the first sign of illness for a full report on your DNA make-up.

Don't worry if the concept of the doshas doesn't make complete sense at first. When I was approached to write this book, the working title was 'Find Your Dosha'. Coming from a practitioner's perspective and knowing how this approach so often causes confusion amongst patients and the general public, I asked if we could put the focus on Agni instead. I believe this is a much easier concept to get to grips with and a better place for all of us to start.

As we take care of our digestive fire and come back into balance, our true prakruti will be revealed, by which time you will feel more confident to read the signs of any future imbalance in your doshas and know how and when to make small adjustments as necessary.

So let's take a closer look now at the three doshas, and make a note of any aspects of Vata, Pitta and Kapha that you feel resonate with you. After spending some time working on looking after your Agni, come back to this chapter again. Do you see any changes? Has your prakruti become clearer?

VATA

Elements: Ether and Air.

Qualities: cold, light, dry, irregular, rough, moving, changeable, clear, quick.

Time of day: 2am to 6am and 2pm to 6pm (when Vata is naturally highest in the body).

Seasons: autumn to early winter (when the weather conditions are most like Vata – windy/dry and cold).

Tastes: pacified by Sweet, Sour and Salty; aggravated by Bitter, Pungent and Astringent.

Key things to remember: Vata is cold, light, dry, rough, clear and mobile (always moving).

Air is characterised as the subtle energy that moves through the Ether and governs biological movement. In this way, Vata governs breathing, blinking of the eyelids, digestion and bowel movements, menstruation, movements in the muscles and tissues, pulsations in the heart and all expansion and contraction and sensory perception. Vata is the dosha responsible for all sensations, feelings and emotions such as self-expression, anxiety, nervousness, stress, fear, pain, tremors and spasms.

Physical characteristics:

We know that Vata is formed of the two elements Ether and Air. But what of Vata's qualities and attributes? How do we *recognise* what Vata might look or feel like in the body? Vata-dominant people tend to have the following physical characteristics:

Body: thin, either very tall or very short, bony, flat- or small-chested.

Face: small eyes, long, pointed tongue, long or pointed nose, brittle teeth, thin, dry lips.

Skin: prone to dryness, very little body hair. Feels the cold easily.

Appetite: variable – can skip meals.

Digestion: irregular/prone to gas and bloating.

Bowel movements: can be irregular. Dislikes going to the toilet anywhere other than at home.

Menstruation: light, short – can be irregular. Prone to anxiety and feeling emotional in lead up to period.

Emotions: prone to anxiety, panic attacks and feeling insecure. Vata-dominant types are often highly creative, sometimes quite spiritual and very sociable (try getting a Vata to stop talking once they get going!). An excess of Vata can mean forgetfulness, being disorganised and lacking willpower.

Vata is the friend who loves to talk, the one who is first on the dance floor and the last to leave. A high-energy chatterbox with a big dose of creativity, Vata loves to try new things and will probably talk you into whatever yoga/art/dance/music class they plan to try next. All that nervous energy means they can get a bit anxious and might not sleep so well.

They are not interested in food in the way that Pitta and Kapha are. They can take it or leave it as their appetites tend to be erratic and they don't like the feeling of being too weighed down with heavy foodstuffs. Vatas are like butterflies – they need to be free to flutter and fly! We all need a Vata friend to keep our spirits light.

Vata people are also like birds: they like to be free and to feel light. According to the principle of 'like attracts like', they therefore enjoy foods that are similar in quality to Vata (remember their light, dry, rough and cold qualities?), so foods like quinoa, oats, raw foods, juices, salads – which have qualities of being dry, light, cold and rough. These are, in fact, precisely the kind of foods you need to avoid having too frequently if you feel you have an imbalance of Vata or if you feel you are a predominantly Vata-type person.

Typical Vata conditions:

An excess of Vata in the body can lead to some of the following common conditions: anxiety, panic attacks, hyperactivity, palpitations, tinnitus, dizziness, insomnia and difficulties sleeping, dry skin/eczema, constipation, and bloating.

A lack of Vata in the body can lead to symptoms such as lethargy and poor circulation.

Some of the common factors that will contribute to creating an imbalance of Vata in the body include:

- excessive consumption of foods that have similar properties to the Vata dosha such as dry, cold, light or rough foods: oats, quinoa, cold salads, raw vegetables, beans. Or excessive intake of foods that are bitter, pungent and astringent in taste;
- inadequate quantities of food, fasting, excessive weight loss;
- excessive exercise;
- inadequate sleep; not sleeping at night and sleeping during the day;
- irregular eating times;
- excessive talking and laughing;
- prolonged exposure to loud music or loud sounds;
- suppression of natural urges such as hunger, thirst, urination, yawning, burping and flatulence;
- horse riding;
- excessive fast travel (trains, planes and fast cars!);
- too much time spent alone in meditation or isolation or looking at electronic devices;
- exposure to cold, dry and windy conditions.

Top tips for treating Vata imbalances:

The above list may seem complex at first. What's wrong with exercise or foods such as quinoa, salad and raw vegetables? But this is where Ayurveda is so unique in its approach. Remember the saying 'one person's medicine is another person's poison'? In the same way that a raw food diet and marathon running might work for one person with no ill effects, this doesn't mean the same will go for you. *Listen to your body.*

If you think you are strongly Vata or have a Vata imbalance, ask yourself about the qualities and attributes of the foods you consume most regularly and the lifestyle you lead. Does it have similar properties of light, cold and rough, like Vata? Have you been rushing around like the whirlwind Vata in the bridge-building story? If so, turn to the opposite qualities. Have something warming, a little heavier and with some lubrication (e.g. olive oil, coconut oil, ghee). Remember the Vata bridge-builder and how much better she felt after a sit down!

Vata Agni will be irregular – so check the sections 'My Top Five Tips to Balance Your Agni' and 'Home Remedies to Balance Your Agni' on page 30 and pages 32–4. The use of culinary herbs and spices in your food will help to further aid Vata's irregular digestion and remove toxins that have built up in the first place by stimulating your digestive fire and natural elimination process. Also:

- Increase foods in your diet that are sweet, sour and salty and have opposite qualities to Vata, such as mashed potato, broths, soups, butter, milk and creamy foods.
- Eat warm, cooked foods and avoid cold drinks, especially those with ice.

- Dress appropriately and wear a scarf, hat, warm socks and gloves in cold weather to stop the body being aggravated by the cold.
- Apply warm oil to the body before bathing.
- Use lubrication both internally and externally. Taking the Ayurvedic herb triphala can help things internally, while massaging the body with a heavy and nourishing oil such as sesame oil or mahanarayan oil will help it externally.
- Wrap the body with clothes to encourage sweating or encourages sweating through a gentle steam bath.
- Eat spices that have a warming effect, such as ginger or black pepper, in order to induce heat.
- Enjoy soothing activities such as singing, listening to gentle music, taking a stroll, spending time with children, non-competitive activities and being outdoors in nature.

PITTA

Elements: Fire and Water.

Qualities: oily, penetrating, sharp, hot, light, spreading and liquid.

Time of day: 10am to 2pm and 10pm to 2am (when Pitta is naturally highest in the body).

Seasons: late spring to summer (when the weather conditions are most like Pitta – hot and sharp).

Tastes: pacified by Sweet, Bitter and Astringent; aggravated by Sour, Salty and Pungent.

Key things to remember: Pitta is hot, sharp, penetrating and oily.

Pitta governs our metabolism and powers of digestion, working to differentiate the helpful parts of nutrition from the waste. It also allows us the power of intellect, processing thoughts and information as well as determining truth and reality. Emotions relating to egotism, anger and controlling behaviours are signs of an imbalanced Pitta.

When it comes to digestion, if Pitta is too low you may experience a loss of appetite, whereas if this dosha is too high it can create heartburn, acid reflux and a need to eat very frequently. Many skin conditions are a sign of aggravated Pitta, including certain types of eczema, acne and rosacea.

Physical characteristics:

Pitta-dominant people tend to have some of the physical characteristics listed below. But remember, just because you may not recognise yourself in these descriptions doesn't mean you can't have an imbalance of Pitta too. Whatever our doshic make-up, we can have an imbalance of one or all three of the doshas, although usually a Pitta-dominant person will tend to suffer more with Pitta-related disorders. (Like increases like!)

Body: medium/average frame and bone structure.

Face: often bright, penetrating eyes, soft gums and moderately sized teeth. Can be prone to early greying and baldness.

Skin: soft and warm, sometimes freckly and prone to being oily.

Appetite: strong - can become excessive when out of balance.

Digestion: in balance, a Pitta person can tolerate large amounts of food well, as their digestion and digestive fire are naturally strong.

Bowel movements: regular - but can become too frequent. Can be prone to 'urgency' in upsetting or stressful situations.

Menstruation: regular with periods that are three to five days long, but which can be prone to be heavier. Can feel irritable in lead up to period.

Emotions: when out of balance, Pitta-dominant types can become self-critical, excessively goal-orientated, jealous, controlling and irritable.

Still trying to visualise Pitta? They love nice things! They don't mind spending money on luxuries such as good clothes and jewellery, and, of course, on pampering themselves and splashing out on 'good' food – your Pitta friend will always choose the steak or lobster and a bottle of Moët from the menu. This means that they can be a bit showy and enjoy the limelight, but Pitta is also hard-working, driven and intelligent, and if they keep those things in balance they can make excellent leaders. Pitta types can be quick to anger and become a bit hot-headed, but they are reliable and get things done. We all need a Pitta friend to indulge in life's luxuries with from time to time!

Typical Pitta conditions:

An excess of Pitta in the body can lead to some of the following common conditions: anger, stress, mouth ulcers, headaches and migraine, hot flushes, acne and rosacea, excessive sweating, irritation of the eyes, hay fever, heavy and/or painful periods and disturbing dreams. It can also create feelings of jealousy, hatred and being goal-obsessed.

So let's take a look at some of the common factors that will contribute to creating an imbalance of Pitta in the body:

· excess consumption of foods that have similar properties to the Pitta dosha, such as hot, sharp, acidic or oily foods or foods that are sour, salty and astringent. These include: tomatoes, fried foods, pickles and fermented foods, mustard, vinegar, chillies, red meat, coffee, cheese and red wine;
· excessive exposure to high-stress situations (in the work place or in relationships);
· being overly controlling and competitive (either with yourself or others);
· an overly hedonistic or luxurious lifestyle;
· incorrect habits such as improper eating and sleeping times;
· eating a large amount of root vegetables such as parsnips, beetroot and carrots – these vegetables spiral their roots into the ground, absorbing heat from the earth that we then take into our bodies when we consume them in big quantities – thereby creating an excess of heat/Pitta;
· excessive use of saunas;
· exposure to very hot conditions, including practices such as Bikram yoga;
· eating when angry or frustrated;
· excessive consumption of alcohol;
· incompatible food combinations. Key ones to avoid would be citrus fruits with dairy, fish and milk, and cooking two types of animal protein together;

- eating too many meals or too frequently during the day;
- too many exotic or citrus fruits such as pineapple, mango, banana, orange and grapefruit (this advice is geared for those of us living in Europe the Northern hemisphere);
- drinking too much caffeine.

Top tips for treating Pitta imbalances:

Firstly, ensure you remove or reduce any of the possible factors listed above and balance your Agni. Aggravated Pitta will often mean the Agni is too high and needs calming down. Check the sections 'My Top Five Tips to Balance Your Agni' and 'Home Remedies to Balance Your Agni' on page 30 and pages 32–4 and take the following steps:

- Consume foods with opposing qualities to Pitta and with sweet, bitter and astringent tastes.
- Spend time outdoors, in nature or walking by water. Seek out cool breezes and shade during the summer months in woods and by the sea.
- Consume a daily glass of cold coriander water to help cool Pitta in the body (see 'Ayurvedic First Aid', page 116).
- Have a coconut-oil massage (either abhyanga, see pages 135–6, or general massage). Coconuts have particular cooling qualities and you may find it helpful to use coconut oil in cooking as well as consuming fresh coconut water.

- Venture out in the moonlight! The moon has special grounding and cooling qualities, so taking a gentle night-time stroll when the moon is out can be very calming for Pitta.
- Enjoy time in the company of those friends and family who are not controlling.
- Be close to water: a river, pond, lake or by the sea. Pitta is made up of the elements of Fire and Water, but Fire often dominates. Spending time close to water helps to address this balance. Gentle, non-competitive swimming is therefore also a good form of exercise for Pitta.
- Experience emotional release. Feelings of jealousy, anger or hatred are often the result of suppressed emotions that we are taught not to express as children. Observing these negative emotions when they occur and learning to practise awareness until the feeling subsides is key to letting go. Just take a deep breath – and let it go.

KAPHA

Elements: Earth and Water.

Qualities: oily/unctuous, cold, heavy, dull, sticky, soft, smooth, static (unmoving).

Time of day: 6am to 10am and 6pm to 10pm (when Kapha is naturally highest in the body).

Seasons: mid-winter to spring (when the weather conditions are most like Kapha: heavy, cold and wet).

Tastes: pacified by Bitter, Pungent and Astringent; aggravated by Sweet, Sour and Salty.

Key things to remember: Kapha is heavy, cold, unctuous, static and smooth.

Kapha helps to lubricate the joints of the body, provide moisture to the skin and heal wounds. It creates the building blocks of our bodies – filling the spaces and giving us biological strength and immunity. It can create emotions of attachment and greed, but in balance it is expressed as calmness, forgiveness and love.

Physical characteristics:

We understand that Kapha is made up of the elements of Earth and Water, but how do we recognise what Kapha might look or feel like in the body? Kapha-dominant people will tend to have some of the following physical characteristics:

Body: full, rounded, heavy-boned, large breasts.

Face: large eyes, thick eyelashes, strong teeth.

Skin: smooth, oily, pale or olive-toned. Hair is lustrous, often dark and wavy.

Appetite: slow and steady.

Digestion: slow.

Bowel movements: can be heavy, though usually regular.

Menstruation: can often last for up to seven days. Usually regular but sometimes has a longer cycle of up to thirty-five days. Can suffer with bloating and swollen breasts in lead up to period.

Emotions: when in balance, Kapha-dominant people are stable, calm and gentle. Prone to heaviness and Kapha-type depression/inertia when Kapha is in excess.

Still trying to visualise Kapha? We all have a Kapha friend (or if you don't you should probably find one)! You know the type – Kaphas like to take care of everyone. You will most likely find Kapha in the kitchen as they love to cook and bake and show they care through food. Kapha *loves* food. Pitta loves 'good' food. Kapha likes *all* food. They are slow, steady and loving. They hate to let anyone down. In balance they are calm, patient and nurturing. Aggravated Kapha will lead to them having difficulty letting go and becoming overly attached to people or things, and their love can become suffocating. They can be lazy (sorry, Kaphas), lack motivation and are prone to holding on to their emotions.

Typical Kapha conditions:

An excess of Kapha in the body can lead to some of the following common conditions: congestion, greasy skin and hair, swelling in feet and ankles, feeling of heaviness, pale skin, drowsiness, lethargy, recurrent coughs and colds.

Decreased Kapha in the body can lead to excessive thirst, dryness of the mouth, dry skin, insomnia and feelings of being overwhelmed or defeated.

So let's take a look at some of the common factors that will contribute to creating an imbalance of Kapha in the body:

- excess consumption of foods that have similar properties to the Kapha dosha, such as heavy, unctuous, sticky or cold foods. These include: cheese, cream, pastries, cakes, desserts, yoghurt, pork and wild meats, raw foods, salads and an excess of starchy foods such as rice and potatoes;
- excessive quantities of food, overeating and indulgence;
- excessive amounts of sleep and sleeping during the day;
- lack of mental stimulation;

- not enough physical exercise or movement, having a sedentary lifestyle;
- experiencing a lot of grief and sadness.

Top tips for treating Kapha imbalances:

As ever, the simple answer to treating an imbalance lies in reducing the factors from the list above, as well as eating foods and adopting practices that have the opposite qualities to Kapha. Remember to check in with your Agni. A Kapha imbalance will usually mean a slow digestive fire. See 'My Top Five Tips to Balance Your Agni' and 'Home Remedies to Balance Your Agni' on page 30 and pages 32–4 to get it fired back up, and take the following steps:

- Increase your intake of foods that are bitter, pungent and astringent.
- Reduce your intake of sweet foods, heavy starch and dairy.
- Enjoy warming foods – and use herbs and spices that will warm and promote digestive fire such as root ginger, cayenne pepper and black pepper.
- Undertake vigorous physical activity (aerobic exercise is particularly good, but take it slowly at first if you aren't used to it or haven't done any in a while).
- Enjoy treatments that involve heat and increased perspiration such as saunas and sunbathing.
- Dry brush and have exfoliating massages (with not too much oil massage).

· Practise intermittent fasting or eating two meals that will sustain you throughout the day, rather than lots of smaller meals or overeating. Digestion is slower in Kapha individuals so they should need to eat less regularly than Vata and Pitta.

The Six Tastes and how they affect the Doshas

Ayurveda places great importance on incorporating all of the six tastes – Sweet, Sour, Salty, Bitter, Pungent and Astringent – in your diet in order to promote balance of all three doshas.

As previously noted, each dosha is pacified or aggravated by certain tastes. Consuming too much of a particular taste will start to aggravate the dosha. As you will have seen in the chapter 'Agni: Your Fire Power', if you are experiencing an aggravation of a particular dosha you might find your body intuitively craves a particular taste. Listen to your body and seek out some of that taste. If the feeling passes, then you know this was a 'healthy' craving. If the craving persists for many days, this is a sign that the craving has become 'unhealthy' and something needs to be done to address the balance.

Remember:

Vata is pacified by Sweet, Sour and Salty; aggravated by Bitter, Pungent and Astringent.

Pitta is pacified by Sweet, Bitter and Astringent; aggravated by Sour, Salty and Pungent.

Kapha is pacified by Bitter, Pungent and Astringent; aggravated by Sweet, Sour and Salty.

Take, for example, the days leading up to your period. Around seven days before your period comes your progesterone levels peak. This is a time of high Pitta!

The heat is rising in the blood and once our period arrives, the heat leaves our bodies and calm descends once more. Because of this high Pitta time, you may find you are particularly drawn to those three tastes that help to calm Pitta – namely Sweet, Bitter and Astringent. Our body sends a signal, we sense the craving and reach for ice cream (Sweet), coffee (Bitter) and wine (Astringent). The right tastes but perhaps not the best choices! It is important to try to choose the right type of foods to satisfy any cravings you might have. Some slices of apple sprinkled with a little cinnamon and put under the grill, or a few dates, for example, would be kinder to your body and your Agni than the bowl of ice cream or chocolate. A handful of pomegranate seeds might likewise be a better solution to an Astringent craving than tucking into a bottle of wine.

If the craving for something sweet is particularly strong, however, you can also experiment with increasing your intake of foods with the opposite qualities, such as a Bitter taste. Try dipping your finger into some raw cacao powder when you are craving something sweet – it actually shocks your tongue into feeling more satisfied!

This again takes us back to the principle of 'like increases like'. We are often drawn to the tastes that relate to the strongest dosha within our bodies. For example, a Kapha-dominant person will enjoy consuming Sweet, Sour and Salty tastes and naturally gravitate towards those. To stay in balance, it is important to be mindful of this and ensure that enough of the other three tastes are consumed – in the case of Kapha, that means Bitter, Pungent and Astringent.

Here are some examples of where to find these tastes:

Sour is found in lemon, lime, tamarind, vinegars, pickled and fermented foods.

Astringent is found in green grapes, pomegranates, cranberries, green beans, alfalfa sprouts and okra.

Pungent is prominent in hot chillies, ginger, onions, garlic, mustard and hot spices.

Bitter is found in rocket, raw cacao, many leafy vegetables, fenugreek and turmeric.

Sweet is prominent in foods such as wheat, rice, dairy, cereals, dates, pumpkins, maple syrup, cinnamon and liquorice root.

Salty is found in sea vegetables, sea salt, tamari, black olives, Himalayan and rock salt.

Daily Dosha Care

You can begin to manage your stress levels, sleep patterns, energy and mental well-being with a few simple Ayurvedic practices. While the guidelines that follow in this chapter are organised into sections for each dosha, they are in fact interchangeable. I recommend that you read up on all three doshas, as imbalances will come and go with different seasons and times of life. Knowing how to recognise these will help you to live healthily and happily! If, for example, you sense that you are usually more strongly Pitta but start feeling some of the symptoms of Kapha imbalance in the middle of winter, follow some of the advice from the Kapha section until the symptoms subside.

And what nicer way is there to begin your daily dosha care than with a warming cup of chai?

MY MORNING RITUAL CHAI TO GENTLY WARM YOUR AGNI (FOR ALL DOSHAS)

I first posted this recipe on Instagram when I was describing how I enjoy the ritual of making it during the autumn and winter months. The simple act of preparing the tea is my morning mindfulness practice, while the warming spices help to gently nurture my body in the colder months by giving me a boost of energy. I have tweaked the blend until the flavour tastes 'just right' for me, but you can play around with the quantities and see what suits you best. It contains many of the spices I have listed as being good for balancing Agni, so you can reap all the benefits of consuming them. It's a great little fire-starter to keep your Agni happy, and a delicious and comforting drink to replace your usual tea or coffee in colder months.

25g/1oz peeled root ginger
10 cardamom pods, lightly bashed
4 whole cloves
½ cinnamon stick (or 1 tsp ground cinnamon)
500ml/17fl oz water
2 ordinary black tea bags
500ml/17fl oz milk or almond milk

brown sugar or jaggery to taste (don't use honey as it should never be heated according to Ayurveda)

Place the ginger, cardamom, cloves and cinnamon in a saucepan with the water and bring to the boil.

Reduce to a simmer and add the tea bags and milk. Simmer very gently for around 5 minutes to infuse the flavours.

Remove from the heat and add sugar to taste (I usually add 1 tsp).

Serve immediately or keep warm for later. This recipe makes around 4 cups, so I usually pour the rest into a flask to enjoy later in the day.

Vata

VATA

Creating a calming routine for the start and end of the day can be especially balancing for Vata, as this dosha is particularly prone to being a bit chaotic and disorganised. If you are feeling any of the symptoms of too much Vata, while an element of routine will benefit you, don't try to set the bar too high. Remember, if you have a lot of Vata you will naturally struggle to stick to a rigid routine anyway, so don't be hard on yourself – start slowly and gently.

MORNING RITUALS FOR BALANCING VATA AND CREATING CALM

If you are usually up with the birds and rushing around, doing a million things before dashing out to the school run/work/the gym (possibly on an empty stomach), try to think mindfully about slowing things down! Replace going for a run or doing intense workouts with some gentle yoga or Pilates. If this seems an inconceivable thing to do at first, just start slowly. Begin by replacing one or two of your usual weekly workouts with something calmer such as yoga, walking or swimming. Just remember to try and take everything at a slower pace and take time to *breathe*!

Morning Meditation: Alternate nostril breathing

1. Begin your morning with some gentle breathwork or meditation. Five or ten minutes is all you need. If you find it hard to sit still for that length of time, build up to this gradually. If you already meditate, try not to do this in excess as it can aggravate Vata.
2. Find a quiet spot in the house. Light a candle or some incense to set the mood. Sit comfortably on the floor, using cushions and blankets to keep you warm, and close your eyes.
3. Place the middle finger of your right hand over your third-eye chakra (the space between your eyebrows).
4. Cover your right nostril with your thumb and breathe deeply through your left nostril for a count of four. Hold the breath for a second or two, release the thumb from the right nostril and cover the left one using your little finger. Breathe out through your right nostril for a count of four. Pause.

5. Breathe in through the right nostril, hold for a moment, then release the little finger from your left nostril and cover the right nostril with your thumb. Breathe out through the left nostril. Pause.
6. Now, breathe in through the left nostril and adjust your fingers to breathe out through the right nostril, pausing to hold the breath as before. Continue this practice, alternating between the two nostrils with slow and steady breaths.
7. Imagine yourself firmly rooted to the ground and visualise a gentle, warm energy flowing through you. You are calm, you are nurtured, you are strong. The Universe is holding you and won't let you fall.

Breakfast

Vata appetite is often erratic. Sometimes you might simply forget to eat or perhaps you just don't fancy eating much. Caffeine is problematic for Vata and therefore best avoided. If you usually have coffee instead of food in the morning, try replacing this with a warm smoothie made with the following deeply nourishing ingredients, which will balance and ground you at the start of the day.

WARM DATE AND ALMOND SMOOTHIE

Soak 5 whole almonds overnight. It is important to soak the almonds so they are more easily digestible.

Blend with 1 cup of *warm* milk (either cow's, coconut or almond milk), 3 dates and a pinch of cinnamon and nutmeg. Don't skip the spices – they will help to gently warm your body and wake up your Agni.

Serve warm.

You may find this smoothie is enough or that you need something more filling, such as Ayurvedic Rice Porridge.

AYURVEDIC RICE PORRIDGE

As dry, rough foods such as muesli, granola and porridge oats are off the table (they will aggravate Vata), an excellent alternative is Ayurvedic rice porridge. (We call it rice 'pudding' in my house because that way the kid eats it too ... !) This also makes for a good breakfast for Pitta people.

Simmer a portion of white basmati rice in milk with a generous pinch of cinnamon, cardamom, nutmeg and grated root ginger for 10–15 minutes until well cooked and a little mushy.

You can add some tinned coconut milk or coconut cream at the end of cooking and stir through for extra creaminess.

Add a small amount of jaggery, maple syrup or brown sugar if it requires sweetening and eat warm.

FIND BALANCE DURING THE DAY

Make a conscious effort to build in time to take five. Draw on the calming effects of your morning breathwork. If it feels as though the day is getting on top of you, practising a few minutes of that gentle breathing exercise (see pages 79–80) will help to bring calm. Even just closing your eyes for a few moments and *remembering* how it felt to sit calmly, warmly and comfortably, taking those deep breaths, will bring some peace.

EAT TO STAY BALANCED

Try not to skip meals or ignore hunger. It is important to eat at regular times to keep Vata balanced. If you feel hungry, a glass of water or a cup of tea won't help – this will only serve to 'dampen' and weaken your Agni. Take notice of the feeling of hunger and eat accordingly; ideally, this should be something cooked and warm with some culinary herbs and spices to aid digestion.

EVENING RITUALS TO RELAX AND HELP YOU SLEEP

The evening wind-down is especially important to calm an overactive Vata mind. Try to ensure that you stick to a regular bedtime and start your wind-down at least thirty minutes before you plan to go to bed. Switch off phones, laptops and the television, and allow yourself time for some calming activities to relax the body and mind.

For example, why not treat yourself to a calming foot massage with some soothing oils just before bed? In Ayurveda, we often use sesame oil for its heavier and grounding properties. Massaging your feet with oil before bed creates a sense of relaxation and grounding that helps bring down anxiety and 'Vata' energy from the head.

The second thing to try is a drink of warm milk (almond milk is lovely) with a pinch of cinnamon, cardamom and nutmeg. All these spices are known to soothe the mind and nutmeg is particularly calming for sleep. If you are feeling especially wired at bedtime, try stirring through ¼ teaspoon of organic ghee into the milk mixture with a pinch of sugar, as this will further help to calm the Vata energy.

Pitta

PITTA

Introducing a manageable yet calming routine at the start and end of the day can be very balancing for Pitta, as this dosha is prone to being rather rigid and stressed. If you are feeling any of the symptoms of too much Pitta, a calming ritual will bring some balance to the beginning of your day. Remember – don't make this another thing you have to do perfectly. Go with the flow.

MORNING RITUALS FOR BALANCING PITTA AND CREATING CALM

If you are a very Pitta person, you probably need to start the day in as organised a way as possible. Sometimes this is out of your control and might lead to feelings of stress. If there is a lot of traffic on your usual route to work or the train is delayed, for example, or something doesn't quite go as you would like or expect, these incidents can throw you off balance. So, at the start of every morning, I want you to avoid looking at your phone or emails upon waking. Instead, set the tone for the day ahead by spending the first ten to fifteen minutes doing some meditation and breathwork so you start the day calmly.

Say to yourself, 'Today things may not always go as I would like or have planned, but I will embrace any difficulties that come my way and take them in my stride'. You cannot control everything all of the time. Just trust and let go. You are cool, calm and collected.

Mornng Meditation: Left nostril breathing

1. Left-nostril breathing is especially effective for calming Pitta. You can call on this breathing technique in short bursts at any point during the day if you feel emotions rising and getting the better of you.
2. Find a quiet spot in the house. Light a candle or some incense to set the mood. Sit comfortably on the floor, using cushions and blankets to keep you warm, and close your eyes.
3. Place the middle finger of your right hand over your third-eye chakra (the space between your eyebrows). With your right hand, cover your right nostril with your thumb and breathe deeply through your left nostril for a count of four. Hold the breath for a second or two.
4. Now cover the left nostril with your little finger and release your thumb. Release the breath slowly through the right nostril for a count of four. Pause.
5. Change the position of your finger and thumb to continue inhaling through the left nostril and exhaling through the right nostril with slow and steady breaths.
6. Imagine yourself firmly rooted to the ground, and visualise a cooling energy flowing through you.

Breakfast

Pitta appetite is strong and you will need to start the day with a nourishing breakfast. Ayurvedic Rice Porridge (see page 81) is a good choice for Pitta too as it won't create excess heat like oats and granola (which would be like adding kindling to the Pitta flames). Eggs are fine a few times a week but can be heating so avoid in excess. If you have them with bread, try to choose a bread that doesn't contain added commercial yeast, as this can be too heating. Sourdough bread is better as it is made from the wild yeast in flour and water. Avoid condiments such as Marmite, honey and peanut butter as these are also aggravating to Pitta. Butter, jam or almond butter are better alternatives. Coffee and green tea are best avoided or kept to an absolute minimum. Choose herbal tea, ordinary tea with milk or the Morning Ritual Chai recipe on page 77 as a compromise for skipping coffee.

FIND BALANCE DURING THE DAY

Make a conscious effort to build in time to take five. Eat lunch away from your desk and step outside at some point for a short walk, even if it is just for ten minutes. Draw on the calming effects of your morning breathwork. If it feels as though the day is getting on top of you, a few minutes of repeating this gentle breathing exercise will help to bring calm.

EAT TO STAY BALANCED

When hunger comes, don't suppress it with coffee. Have a small snack – some dates or almonds, for example. Eat a warm, cooked lunch: dals, stews, cooked vegetables with rice and a little white meat or fish or even a jacket potato are all filling options to keep Pitta satisfied. If you like soup but find it is not always filling enough, add a tin of chickpeas (whole or blended in) for some extra protein. If you feel your hunger is excessive, try balancing your digestive fire by taking some roasted cumin and honey before meals (see page 33 for the method).

EVENING RITUALS TO RELAX AND HELP YOU SLEEP

Pittas usually fall asleep pretty well but can be disturbed by lucid dreams. Ensure you allow yourself time to properly wind down before bed. Avoid heavy exercise in the evening or eating too late at night if you can. Turn off your phone, laptop and television at least thirty minutes before you plan to go to bed. A foot or head massage with some cooling coconut oil is beneficial for Pitta types to induce a calm night of sleep. You may find it helpful to journal and write down your thoughts at the end of each day. This is another helpful practice in beginning to let go of those things you have no control over. Spend five minutes reflecting on the day – and be gentle and forgiving to yourself if not everything went as you would have liked.

Kapha

KAPHA

Where the other two doshas need calming activities, Kaphas need something to invigorate them and warm up their system so that they can get going in the day. If you are a very Kapha person, morning is a good time to get some movement into your daily regime to give yourself some energy for the day ahead. Dancing along to an online dancercise video, going for a short jog around the park, taking part in a spin class or any kind of activity that you can commit to doing a few mornings a week will help to keep Kapha in balance. Try to exercise before you eat. Ideally, you shouldn't engage in excess activity after eating as this is when your Agni needs all its energy to work on digesting food.

MORNING RITUALS FOR BALANCING KAPHA AND CREATING ENERGY

Kapha types may be inclined to stay in bed longer than necessary or oversleep, so I encourage you to wake up at around 6am, before the 'Kapha time' of 6am to 10am sets in, when it will become harder for you to get motivated!

Start the day with some dry body brushing or garshana. This invigorating dry-brushing technique is great for alleviating excess Kapha, stimulating the skin and helping to eliminate toxins. You can perform this every morning as part of your Kapha-balancing daily rituals or whenever you feel you may have an imbalance of Kapha. Depending on your dosha, the time of year and any symptoms of imbalance, you may want to do some dry brushing first and then apply an oil and perform abhyanga massage (see pages 135–6). In winter, for example, you may find your body needs the extra stimulation of garshana as well as some nourishment from oil massage to counteract any cold or dryness.

How to Perform Garshana

Performing garshana at least four or five times a week will help to alleviate a slow and sluggish Kapha system.

You will need a dry body brush or some exfoliating gloves.

Starting at your feet and ankles, and making sure always to brush upwards towards the heart, sweep from the ankle of your left leg up the back of that leg to the top of your buttocks. Repeat five times and then do the same on your right leg.

Brush each buttock in a circular movement five times. Make circular motions in a clockwise direction over your stomach for five rounds.

Now work on your arms: make five long strokes upwards from your left wrist up to the top of your left shoulder (always brushing upwards towards the heart). Then repeat on the right arm. Now make small circular movements with the brush and massage in an upward direction from your left hand to left shoulder and over the chest. Repeat on the right arm and chest.

Morning Meditation: Right nostril breathing

1. Kaphas are advised to perform right-nostril breathing to bring energy and warmth to the body. You can call on this breathing technique in short bursts at any point in the day when you feel you need to energise yourself.
2. Place the middle finger of your right hand over your third-eye chakra (the space between your eyebrows). With your right hand, cover your left nostril with your little finger and breathe deeply through your right nostril for a count of four. Hold the breath for a moment.
3. Now cover the right nostril with your thumb and release your little finger. Release the breath through the left nostril for a count of four. Pause.
4. Continue to inhale through the right nostril and exhale through the left nostril with slow, steady breaths, adjusting your fingers accordingly.
5. Imagine an uplifting energy flowing through you.

Breakfast

A light, warm breakfast such as some stewed fruits (apples, pears, berries with a pinch of cinnamon, nutmeg, cloves, ginger and cardamom) is a delicious option for Kaphas. So too are slices of pineapple, sprinkled with a little brown sugar and placed under the grill for a few minutes until browned.

INVIGORATE YOURSELF DURING THE DAY

If you have a desk-based job or sedentary lifestyle, make a conscious effort to bring more movement into your day. Try to get up at regular intervals and move around – shake it off, stretch out and go for a five-minute walk around the block, or even just walk up and down the stairs a couple of times.

Once or twice a week, find ways to change up your routine. Try something new for lunch, take a different route to work, sign up for a new class or hobby, put in a date to meet up with a friend you haven't seen for a while. Remember that too much Kapha can feel like a heaviness or inertia. Changing up your routine every once in a while is therefore helpful for Kapha to avoid getting stuck in a rut.

EATING TO STAY BALANCED

In terms of eating, you may find it helpful to have your main meal at lunchtime and something lighter in the evening. Alternatively, you may find that you feel better if you eat twice rather than three times a day. If so, choosing heavier grains and protein to keep you sustained and foods that release slow-burning energy are the best options for you. Digestion can be slow in a Kapha-dominant person, so be careful not to overeat out of habit. Tune in to your body and only eat if there is true hunger. Hunger is a sign that your Agni is awake and ready to receive food.

EVENING RITUALS TO RELAX AND CREATE FOCUS FOR THE FOLLOWING DAY

Kaphas don't tend to need much help in getting to sleep. However, as with the other doshas, I always advise trying to create a regular bedtime routine and switching off electronic devices at least thirty minutes before you intend to go to sleep. Try to ensure you have spent a few minutes organising anything you need for the next day so that you don't have an easy excuse not to have a light warming breakfast or get some exercise in! Spend five minutes with your diary or journal and set yourself some long-term and short-term goals – things you would like to see and do: perhaps a show at the theatre, learning a new skill or reading a new book. Keep a journal every evening to reflect back and make sure you are doing something to work towards these enjoyable goals. Don't get caught in a cycle of putting things off!

Food as
Medicine

Today, we are rediscovering what our ancestors knew many thousands of years ago: that food is one of the most powerful medicines we have.

A Short History of Medicine

2001 BC	Here, eat this root.
1000 AD	That root is heathen. Here, say this prayer.
1850 AD	That prayer is superstition. Here, drink this potion.
1920 AD	That potion is snake oil. Here, swallow this pill.
1945 AD	That pill is ineffective. Here, take this penicillin.
1955 AD	Oops ... the bugs have mutated. Here, take this tetracycline.
1960–1999 AD	Thirty-nine more 'oops' ... Here, take this more powerful antibiotic.
2020 AD	The bugs have won! Here, eat this root.

Kitchen-cupboard Essentials

Growing up in the south of England in the 1990s, if I had a stomach bug I would be given a dose of kaolin and morphine from a little brown bottle. Headaches and fevers would be treated with Calpol and when we all overindulged at Christmas, Mum would pass round the Rennie and Gaviscon antacids. Later in life, as I discovered Ayurveda and met friends who had grown up in India, Sri Lanka and other parts of the world, I marvelled at the differences in approach to some of these common ailments. Instead of reaching for the medicine cabinet, their parents would go to the kitchen cabinet. And more specifically – the spice rack! With just a few simple ingredients, you can quickly and easily make your own natural Ayurvedic home remedies to help ease a number of minor but common disorders.

Here are a few of my favourites to keep in the cupboard at home. I encourage you to experiment with them and incorporate more of these key ingredients into your diet and cooking so that you can reap their benefits and correct imbalances.

GHEE

Ghee is one of Ayurveda's most treasured foods – and for good reason, as ghee is said to be the closest thing we have to the substance of Ojas. It should not be confused with the simpler clarified butter, because ghee is simmered at much lower temperatures to ensure all its wonderful nutrients are retained. Use a small amount in your cooking (like any fat, too much can increase cholesterol) and enjoy a dose of omega-3 and omega-9 essential fatty acids along with vitamins A, D, E and K.

Look for ghee that is organic, ideally from grass-fed cows, and made using slow, traditional methods.

FENUGREEK

These little seeds are a handy kitchen staple. They are bitter in taste, so including them in your cooking is an easy way to include this vital flavour, which is often missing from our diets. Fenugreek has also been found to contain a compound called 4-hydroxyisoleucine, which works to help normalise blood glucose levels – another great reason to make this little seed a regular in your home cooking.

AJWAIN SEEDS (ALSO KNOWN AS CAROM)

These are another mighty little seed I couldn't be without. They have a slightly pungent and bitter taste (so again, a little in cooking can be useful for balancing the six tastes) and have been found to be very helpful in easing various digestive complaints.

CUMIN

These small, brownish seeds are truly my kitchen-cupboard saviour and are rich in copper, iron, antioxidants, vitamins A and C, zinc and potassium. They contain compounds that boost digestive enzymes and saliva, meaning that cumin will help you to digest your food more easily (by helping your Agni!). Experiment with adding a pinch to savoury dishes.

CORIANDER SEEDS

Rich in antioxidants, coriander seeds have exceptional cooling properties, which makes them especially helpful for Pitta problems.

ROOT GINGER

Supportive to all three doshas, ginger is a gently warming spice and therefore has a good effect on the Agni. It is often recommended that you chew a little ginger with a pinch of salt and a squeeze of lime before meals to boost your Agni if it is low. Despite its warming qualities, ginger is one of the only rhizomes that won't overly aggravate Pitta (though it should be noted that ground ginger has different properties and should be used more sparingly by Pitta types).

CLOVES

Cloves possess antimicrobial qualities. You can also try crushing a few whole cloves between the teeth and inhaling the aromas to help a coughing fit.

COCONUT OIL

The lauric acid in coconut oil helps support and build the immune system. Virgin coconut oil happens to have the highest concentration of lauric acid outside of mother's milk, making this potent fatty acid an important ally in supporting a healthy immune system with its antiviral properties. Its cooling properties are particular helpful for inflammatory Pitta conditions.

TURMERIC

Modern and ancient medicine have long praised turmeric's benefits. It's a potent anti-inflammatory and antioxidant, but there is so much conflicting advice on how best to use and consume this powerful root, ranging from consuming whole tablespoons of turmeric powder to late-night lattes and cold-pressed turmeric root juices for breakfast.

Ayurveda teaches us that taking a single active ingredient (which is the basis of so many preparations in Western medicine) is not what nature intended. This is how 'side effects' occur. In Ayurveda, we instead place an importance on understanding the particular qualities of any food or herb. Turmeric has drying and heating qualities which, if consumed incorrectly, may exacerbate many disorders that in Ayurveda contribute to excess heat or dryness in the body (heat = Pitta, dryness = Vata). To counteract these qualities, turmeric should be combined with something unctuous like ghee or coconut milk (these have Kapha qualities which then create a balance) and ideally with cooling spices such as cinnamon, cumin and ground coriander when cooking curries, vegetables and lentils. In this way, the body can safely harness the benefits of turmeric without creating any excess dryness or heat. Because of turmeric's heating and drying nature, Vata and Pitta types should consume small amounts, while Kapha types can afford to enjoy it more frequently.

BLACK PEPPER

A small pinch of black pepper will aid digestion of heavy or oily foods.

CINNAMON

Antibacterial, antifungal and antimicrobial, cinnamon can play a part in reducing 'bad' cholesterol (low-density lipoproteins, or LDL) and increasing 'good' cholesterol (high-density lipoproteins, or HDL). Research suggests it can also help to reduce blood sugar levels. Enjoy a generous pinch on stewed fruits, in rice porridge or to perk up your tea.

CARDAMOM

Cardamom brings gentle sweetness and contains many essential vitamins and minerals, but most importantly, a dose of iron, which will help to bring relief to fatigue and weakness.

NUTMEG

This spice has a particularly calming effect and is therefore helpful for those who suffer from anxiety or insomnia. It is traditionally used in Ayurveda to help aid a restful night's sleep, so one of the best ways to take it is in a little warm milk at bedtime. A generous pinch will do.

Ayurvedic First Aid

During the course of this book, we have looked at the importance of eating the right foods, having a balanced Agni and building our Ojas. We have discovered how, together, these three things form the blueprint for a healthy body and mind. As with all things in life, there will be times where this approach works well for you and other times when you might still struggle to stay balanced. It happens to the best of us and is just part of life's natural ebbs and flows. In this chapter, I have put together some further tips and advice on how to manage certain ailments that might strike at different times, so you can feel empowered to treat these naturally.

For Gut Health

In addition to the suggestions listed below, see 'My Top Five Tips to Balance Your Agni on page 30.

HEARTBURN AND ACID REFLUX

Soak ½ tsp of fenugreek seeds in a small cup of hot water and drink after your meal.

CONSTIPATION

Warm 100ml/3½fl oz or so of cow's or almond milk in a pan with a pinch of cinnamon, nutmeg and cardamom and stir in ½ tsp of organic ghee and a pinch of sugar. Adding a teaspoon of Triphala powder (an Ayurvedic herbal remedy which is widely available in health food stores) along with the ghee will gently and effectively ease constipation by lubricating the colon and calming Apana Vata.

NAUSEA, GASTRITIS, CONSTIPATION, TRAPPED WIND AND INDIGESTION

Toast a pinch or two of ajwain seeds (also known as carom) in a dry frying pan over a moderate heat for a minute or so until fragrant. Set one cupful of water to boil in a pan and add ½ tsp of the toasted seeds. Simmer gently for 5–10 minutes until the water becomes a light-brown tea colour. Strain the seeds and sip the water slowly until you get relief. NB: Don't drink this brew if you have diarrhoea!

AFTER A STOMACH UPSET

Heat a cupful of water in a pan along with 4–5 whole cloves. Simmer gently for 10 minutes. Remove from the heat, strain and allow to cool a little. Take small sips of this soothing oral rehydration solution until symptoms subside.

For Hangovers and Muscle Pain

TO TREAT A HANGOVER

Add the juice of ½ lime to a glass of warm water. Add a pinch of salt, ½ tsp of sugar and ½ tsp of bicarbonate of soda and drink.

TO TREAT MUSCLE PAIN

Soaking in a warm bath with ⅔ cup of baking soda and ¼ cup of ground ginger will help to ease cold, aching muscles.

For Colds and Flu

Root ginger is your saviour here! The following ginger and coriander remedy was generously shared with me by the wonderful Dr Wathsala at The Ayurvedic Clinic, and will help ease symptoms of flu and colds as well as coughs and runny noses.

HOT GINGER AND CORIANDER WATER

Set 2–3 cups of water to boil in a pan. Add 3 tsp of whole coriander seeds (there's no need to crush them). Simmer for around 6 minutes and then add 2–3 slices of fresh root ginger and simmer for a further 2 minutes. Add a little sugar to taste if you wish. Strain and drink warm up to 3 times a day. Always make this water fresh each day.

INFUSION FOR TONSILLITIS AND SORE THROATS

Crush 1 garlic clove into a cup of boiled water. Add a slice of ginger, a squeeze of lime and 2 tsp salt. Steep for a few minutes while the water cools and then gargle with the mixture. Repeat this process throughout the day. I have stopped many a bout of tonsillitis in its tracks using this remedy on friends and family!

COLD CORIANDER WATER FOR MILD UTIS

Lightly crush 3 tsp of coriander seeds and add to a glass with 200ml/7fl oz of cool water or coconut water. Leave overnight, strain and drink on an empty stomach. As well as treating mild cases of urinary tract infections such as cystitis, this is great for cooling aggravated Pitta.

For Mouth Ulcers and Anaemia

MOUTH ULCERS CAUSED BY STRESS

Mix ½ tsp of organic ghee with a little ground turmeric. Apply this paste to the ulcer a few times per day. You can also make an antibacterial mouthwash with whole cloves: set a cupful of water in a pan to boil along with 4 or 5 whole cloves. Simmer gently for 10 minutes. Remove from the heat, strain and allow to cool a little. Then swill around the mouth for one minute and spit out. Repeat regularly until ulcers subside.

FOR SYMPTOMS OF ANAEMIA

Try gently crushing 2 or 3 cardamom pods in a cup of milk and warm in a saucepan for a few minutes. Allow the milk to infuse with the cardamom and drink.

For Skin and Hair

CUMIN WATER

Cumin water is used all over India for everything from creating a clear complexion and shiny hair to supporting the liver. To boost hair and skin health, set one cupful of water to boil in a pan and add 1 tsp of whole cumin seeds. Simmer gently for 5–10 minutes. Remove from the heat, allow to cool, strain and drink on an empty stomach.

COCONUT OIL HAIR MASK

Warm a little oil between your palms and apply to your scalp, then rub it through to the ends of your hair. Leave on overnight – the oil usually absorbs into your hair, but you can place a towel over your pillow or wrap your hair in a towel if you need to. In the morning, massage some shampoo into the hair and scalp before stepping into the shower, then lather and rinse. Coconut gives hair a beautiful shine and lustre when applied in this way once a week.

For Sleep and Calm

RELAXING BEDTIME DRINK

Warm approx. 100ml/3½fl oz of cow's or almond milk in a pan with a pinch of cinnamon, nutmeg and cardamom (all known to help aid restful sleep). Stir in ¼ tsp of organic ghee and a pinch of sugar. Drink before bed to help relax your mind and body and enjoy a peaceful night's sleep.

For Emotional Comfort

If you are in need of emotional comfort, build up your Ojas (see pages 36–43). Try to take the focus away from yourself for a moment and create a calm and gentle environment at home. Cook a meal that you enjoy making or which you know others will enjoy eating, and sit down with your family or friends; or simply appreciate a peaceful dinner in your own company.

Take a moment before you eat to consider something in your life that you feel grateful for and sit with that thought for a few moments before you begin eating. Eat slowly and mindfully and savour the flavours of your food. You will feel a sense of calm and comfort when you can take the time to eat in this way and, with time, your emotional difficulties may start to subside. If necessary, seek professional advice to help you tackle long-lasting emotional problems.

For Work and Relationships

I am afraid that there is no quick and easy home remedy for difficulties at work or in your relationships. Looking after your Agni and building up your Ojas to support yourself will help. I would also encourage you to get well acquainted with the three doshas as described in the chapter 'The Doshas and You'. By better understanding and recognising yourself and those around you through the characteristics of the different doshas, you will better understand what motivates you and others to behave in certain ways.

You can't change these aspects of who you are, but you can learn to accept the strengths and weaknesses that come as part of your doshic make-up. Some people may find that once they start to adopt Ayurveda fully into their life and come into balance, they begin to question the job or relationships they chose when they were out of balance. If you are a Vata individual working in a fast-paced and stressful (read: Pitta) environment in the City, for example, you may start to realise that this does not actually suit you, nor is it good for your health. It takes guts to reach that realisation and it takes even more courage to do something about it.

Relationships are no different. You can improve how you navigate them once you understand your dosha and that of those closest to you, but sometimes it may be necessary to let go of those people or situations that could be detrimental to your balance and lasting well-being. Thinking back to the bridge-building story earlier in this book, you will experience all three of those dosha characters in your life. Perhaps you have a very Kapha-type mother and find her fussing and love (and feeding) become suffocating at times. Perhaps you have a dominant Pitta-type father who can sometimes seem overbearing. You can't change this, but you can better understand the person by understanding their dosha and that, in turn, can bring you some comfort and peace.

Similarly, when choosing a partner for yourself, if you know you are strongly Vata, perhaps you will do best to seek out a Kapha-type to balance you and bring some grounding to your naturally flightier energy. But remember – there is no 'correct' or 'perfect' – only a better understanding of ourselves and each other.

So, just as you will adopt practices and make changes to what you eat, don't be afraid to take that leap of faith and seek balance in every area of your life. If something is causing you an imbalance, sooner or later you will have a choice to make – to accept that it will ultimately impair your health or to be brave enough to make a change. Trust in yourself.

Seasonal
Self-care

Whether you are just beginning your journey into Ayurveda or are an old hand, you will discover how each season (and time of life) brings with it a new set of challenges to your health. By understanding the nature of these, we can feel better equipped and prepared to cope with any adverse effects. However, not only do the doshas govern the seasons but our time of life and even the hours in our day.

The Doshas and the Seasons of Life

Ayurveda divides the average life span into three parts, each of which represents one of the three doshas.

- From birth to around the age of twelve is the KAPHA time of life.
- Once we enter puberty at around twelve, until menopause in our fifties, is the PITTA time.
- The latter years of life from around the age of sixty onwards are our VATA time.

Think of it as the dawn, noon and dusk of our lives: Kapha, Pitta and Vata. These three stages are actually a rather beautiful way of stepping back and seeing the three different doshas at work.

The soft, squidgy body of a young child in their Kapha time of life perfectly represents the Kapha elements of Earth and Water. And what child doesn't like milk, sweet treats, yoghurt, carbs and sweet fruits? We see children delight in all the classic Kapha foods.

And then the hormones arrive with all the great fanfare of a volcano exploding! And your little angel changes overnight into a teenager. The Pitta fire has been lit. Our twenties, thirties and forties are a period of high energy and drive, when the Pitta elements of Water and Fire come into play and energy and ambition come to the fore. For young women this means menstruation begins, perhaps with acne and other hormonal issues accompanying it. As we move into becoming adults our tastes change – we favour Sweet, Bitter and Astringent. When the stress of a family, mortgage or job are hitting us hard, we go hard on those three tastes in their most common forms: chocolate (Sweet), coffee (Bitter) and alcohol (Astringent)!

In our fifties, the Fire starts to die down and leave the body – perhaps with yet another fanfare of a tricky menopause, but hopefully it leaves gently as Vata time sets in. Just because this is the last phase of life, it doesn't have to mean there is no adventure! Remember that Vata is the dosha of movement and creativity. Perhaps the children have grown up and left home, and you feel invigorated by the increase in Vata, so decide that now is the time for new hobbies or activities? Respect this time of your life for all its gentle beauty and remember that principle of 'like increases like'. Don't go too crazy with all the dashing around and new hobbies. Take the time to be still and reflect once a day, and eat warm, nourishing foods. Respect Vata's elements of Air and Ether and you will be able to avoid excessive fragility in later years.

Seasonal Rituals to Keep You Balanced throughout the Year

If you can understand the qualities of each of the Ayurvedic seasons and how they impact the three doshas, you will be better able to navigate any adverse effects the seasons may have on your health and well-being. In Ayurveda, the year is divided into three seasons relating to each of the doshas:

VATA season: mid-autumn to early winter

KAPHA season: midwinter to spring

PITTA season: late spring to early autumn

Our individual prakruti (or doshic DNA) and which time of life we are currently in (childhood, adulthood or old age) will influence how our bodies interact with and respond to each of these seasons. If you are a Pitta-dominant person, in the Pitta time of life in the middle of a hot summer, you are probably going to be feeling some symptoms of aggravated Pitta! But you can still find ways to manage this: balancing your Agni, eating cooling foods, spending time in the shade, near water or doing calming activities will all help to prevent your Pitta from getting out of control.

Here are some general tips for managing each transition throughout the year. Remember there is never a 'one size fits all' in Ayurveda. Each of us is completely unique, so play around with these and find what works for you. Keep in mind the principle of 'like increases like' and look to an opposite quality to bring balance and you will be on the right track.

VATA SEASON

As autumn sets in, the key characteristics of this time of year are cold, dry and windy. The leaves fall from the trees and become dry and crisp underfoot and there is a definite chill in the air. The ground becomes dry and hard. Everything feels that little bit more fragile and delicate – just like Vata in our bodies. If you feel you already have a dominance of Vata, you will need to take extra care during this season to avoid it becoming further aggravated.

Disorders that become more common during Vata season:

- earache
- vertigo
- dry cough
- sore throat
- constipation
- asthma
- Vata-type eczema
- osteoarthritis.

Tips for staying in balance:

- Pay attention to your Agni.
- Keep warm – dress appropriately for the weather conditions, keeping your hands, feet, ears and head cosy.
- Practise abhyanga massage or warm oil massage (see pages 151–52) to stop the body becoming too dry.
- Use ghee and other oils in your cooking to create lubrication on the inside.

- Massage your feet with warm oil before bedtime to ground yourself and bring a sense of calm.
- Avoid light, dry, cold foods such as quinoa, chia seeds, oats, seeds, salads, cold juices, and opt instead for heavier, cooked food with warming spices such as cumin, root ginger, cloves and black pepper.
- Include Sweet, Sour and Salty tastes in your diet and avoid too much Bitter, Astringent and Pungent food and drink.
- Enjoy calming activities such as breathing exercises and gentle yoga. Have a sit down! Avoid excessive physical activity and very loud music.

KAPHA SEASON

Deep mid-winter is the beginning of Kapha season. Kapha qualities of cold, heaviness, lethargy and damp are everywhere to be seen – from boggy fields of muddy earth to the heavy, lead-coloured rainclouds in the sky. But as Kapha season draws to a close, spring begins. And, just like a new baby born to the world, new life grows from the earth. This damp, wet and cold heaviness will disturb Kapha in the body and we often get coughs and colds with more mucous congestion at this time. If you feel you already have a dominance of Kapha, you will need to take extra care during this season to avoid it becoming further aggravated.

Disorders that become more common during Kapha season:

- cough
- cold
- congestion
- chest infections
- asthma
- lethargy
- depression and low mood
- weight gain.

Tips for staying in balance:

- Take care of your Agni.
- If you are Kapha-dominant, avoid the temptation to hibernate and sleep excessively or during the day.

- Eat cooked, warm foods – include plenty of bitter greens in your diet along with digestive spices such as cumin, black pepper and ginger.
- Avoid cold, heavy foods, especially cheese, yoghurt and ice cream.
- You may find it helpful to eat heavier grains and chickpeas to help keep you sustained for longer periods and to have two filling meals a day instead of three.
- Shake up your routine from time to time! Find hobbies or pursuits that take you slightly out of your comfort zone. Challenge yourself mentally and physically a few times a week.

As the weather begins to warm and Pitta arrives, some of the Kapha that has built up in the body will start to 'melt' or liquefy, which is often why we are more susceptible to colds and hay fever at the start of spring.

PITTA SEASON

As we enter late spring and high summer, the earth warms up and Pitta season arrives – with sharp, penetrating light from the sun, scorched earth and heatwaves. Just like our Pitta time of life, summer has energy and exuberance, and seems to stretch out before us with so much promise. If you feel you already have a dominance of Pitta, you will need to take extra care during this season to avoid it becoming further aggravated.

Disorders that become more common during Pitta season:

- hay fever
- inflammatory conditions
- short temper
- heatstroke
- skin rash/hives
- Pitta-type eczema.

Tips for staying in balance:

- Keep your Agni balanced.
- Avoid an excess of Sour, Salty or Pungent food and drinks.
- Avoid chilli, tomatoes and fermented foods.
- Keep alcohol and caffeine intake to a minimum, if possible.
- Avoid getting overheated – this sounds obvious, but look for shade and a cool breeze.
- Find some time to be by the water or in woods and nature.

- Do meditation and breathing exercises – and practise letting go of situations you cannot control.
- Spend time outside in the moonlight if you can because it is very cooling for Pitta!
- Enjoy calming activities such as gentle yoga, breathing exercises and spending time with your loved ones.
- Have cooling foods and drinks – cold coriander water (see page 116) and coconut water are good choices.

How to Perform Abhyanga Massage

This Ayurvedic massage technique is wonderful for calming Vata and Pitta. Once you have tried it, you will soon see why and I'm sure it will become an integral part of your daily routine. It helps to disperse toxins, beat fatigue, calm nerves and leave you feeling balanced and invigorated. What is not to love about caring for yourself and your body with a daily warm oil massage?

- Vata conditions: use warm sesame oil.
- Pitta conditions: use coconut oil.

Warm the oil by placing the container into a bowl of hot water for a few minutes. Then pour a little of the oil into a small bowl or plastic container – around 3–4 tbsp is usually enough.

Dip in your fingertips and lightly apply the oil to your whole body.

Wait a few minutes. Then begin to massage the body with firm sweeping movements, beginning at the ankles and feet and moving upwards. Spend longer on any areas that feel tender or tight.

When you are ready, wrap yourself in a towel or dressing gown and relax for at least ten minutes (or as long as you can). Once or twice a week, find time for a longer period of relaxation to fully reap the benefits of this practice. If you are building an abhyanga massage into your morning routine, this is when you could sit and perform some gentle breathwork or meditation.

Shower off if you wish or simply pat down any excess oil with a paper towel and continue your day.

Trusted Practitioners

Please visit www.theayurvedacoach.com for one-to-one Ayurvedic consultations, herbs, advice and personalised plans with me, Claire. Consultations take place in Surrey, London or anywhere in the world via Zoom and FaceTime.

To find a professional practitioner near you, visit:

The Association of Ayurvedic Professionals UK
www.aapuk.net

Australasian Association of Ayurveda Inc (Australia)
www.ayurved.org.au/

National Ayurvedic Medical Association (US)
www.ayurvedanama.org

If you are interested in learning more about Ayurveda generally, visit the Ayurvedic Institute UK's website www.ayurvedainstitute.co.uk

Acknowledgements

I would like to thank my literary agent Valeria for believing in me and for bringing this opportunity into my life. Thank you to everyone at Penguin Random House for their encouragement, support and expertise throughout the process – to my Editor Sam and to Laura and Muna. Thanks to my wonderful PR team at Whitehair.Co especially Emma, Juliet and Zoja.

I am grateful to all the family and friends, past and present, who have touched my life and been part of my journey to this point. I would like to give special heartfelt thanks to my husband George and my darling daughter Phoebe for their unwavering love and support throughout the writing of this book and always. Thank you George for all the weekends you spent on extra dad duty to allow me time to think and write!! To Stephanie, Jessica and Miriam: Three Vata/Pitta women who inspire me every day and I could never be without.

Finally, I would like to thank everyone at the Ayurveda Institute UK for their tireless work in teaching true and authentic Ayurveda for the benefit of everyone. To Dr Deepika, Ajanta, Melani, Dr Wathsala, Sachi and everyone involved behind the scenes. The minute I first stepped foot in your door I felt like I was home. I kept you all, and your teachings, in my heart while I wrote and I hope I have done you proud.

Index

Notes

_____

_____

_____

_____

_____

_____

_____

_____

_____

_____

_____

_____

_____

_____

_____

_____

_____

_____

_____

_____

_____

_____

_____

_____

_____

_____

_____

Notes

CLAIRE PAPHITIS

Claire Paphitis is The Ayurveda coach. Inspired by her experience of healing through Ayurveda, she studied at The Ayurveda Institute in London before opening her consultation practice in Surrey, UK. She shares ayurvedic advice at theayurvedacoach.com. You can find her on Instagram: @the_ayurveda_coach

MORE NOW AGE ESSENTIALS

BE WILD BE FREE: ESSENTIAL SPIRIT ANIMALS AND GUIDES
by Catherine Björksten

BLOOM & THRIVE: ESSENTIAL HEALING HERBS & FLOWERS
by Brigit Anna McNeill

FIND YOUR FLOW: ESSENTIAL CHAKRAS
by Sushma Sagar

YOU ARE A RAINBOW: ESSENTIAL AURAS
by Emma Lucy Knowles

YOU ARE COSMIC CODE: ESSENTIAL NUMEROLOGY
by Kaitlyn Kaerhart